AF264852

OVERTON

(Caullid yn auncient tyme ORTON MADOC)

IN DAYS GONE BY.

By GEORGE JOHN HOWSON, A.M.

PARSONNE OF YE PAROCHE.

OVERTON

(Caullid yn auncient tyme ORTON MADOC)

IN DAYS GONE BY.

By GEORGE JOHN HOWSON, A.M.

PARSONNE OF YE PAROCHE.

To

Mrs. Peel,

of

Bryn-y-pys.

IMPRINTED AT OSWESTRY
BY
WOODALL AND CO.,
AT THE
CAXTON PRINTING OFFICES.
MDCCCLXXXIII.

preface.

IN sending out this little book, I would entirely disclaim any title to being an antiquary or an archæologist. These pages are merely the outcome of an idea which occurred to me in beginning a Parish Magazine for Overton. They are a chatty description and history of the place in which nearly four years have been happily spent. Accuracy in every detail is not vouched for. Explanation of the strange Anglo-Welsh names of places and fields is only attempted. But I hope that the little volume will not be without an interest of its own to the inhabitants and neighbours of Overton Madoc. My thanks are due to Rev. M. H. Lee, Rev. T. H. G. Puleston, Mr. Askew Roberts, Miss Lloyd Fletcher, and others for the permission to use MSS. and books in their possession, and researches that they have made.

G. J. H.

Overton Rectory,
Christmas, 1883.

CONTENTS.

ILLUSTRATIONS.

CHAPTER I.

Ancient History of Overton.

VERTON Village lies almost in the centre of that part of
Flintshire commonly called Maelor, and on the west edge
of the division called Maelor Saesnag, or English Maelor, as
opposed to Maelor Cymraeg, or Welsh Maelor. The two
divisions belonged to the district called Powysland, that part
of the country originally owned by the Princes of Powys, who received it
in succession from Roderick, King of Wales, A.D., 870. In 1160, Powysland was divided between the two sons of one Meredydd ab Bleddyn ab
Cynvyn.

Madoc, or Madog, the elder, had for his portion Powys Vadoc. This
man had three sons, one of whom, Gruffyth Maelor, received the two Mae-
lors as his inheritance. Powel, in his *History of Wales*, says that in time
the property passed through the hands of Earl Warren, the guardian of a

son of this Gruffyth (which son was treacherously murdered), and the
to Arundell, so to Mowbray, Earl of Norfolk, by whose attainder f
treason it passed to the Crown.

The word Maelor is supposed to signify a traffic place, and this seen
to be a natural title for this district, for it was the border-land over whi
bargains were struck and business transacted.

At the time of the conquest, 1066, it is said Overton was in tl
possession of a Saxon Chieftain, but was granted by the Conqueror,
Robert Fitzhugh, one of his followers. Edward I., in the 14th year of h
reign (1286), gave the lordship to his Queen, Eleanor, who granted it
Robert de Crevecœur, with the privilege of a weekly market and fair.
the 20th year of Edward's reign (1292), he made it a free borough 1
Charter. The same Monarch in the following year (1293) command
Reginald de Grey, Chief-Justice of Chester, to go personally to Overt
and to assign to the burgesses, and such other as might be induced
become inhabitants, competent lands within the demesne of Overt
Castle, and wood to build them burgages and in the 28th year of his rei
(1300), Edward granted to the burgesses, an exemption from toll for sev
years, and various other immunities. Edward II. (1307) gave the borou
and lordship to his Queen, Isabel, and in the 14th year of Edward I.
(1341) they were granted, together with other lands in Maelor, to Eubi
le Strange, Baron of Knockyn, with a confirmation of the precedi
Charter, which was also confirmed and enlarged with additional privileg
in the 20th year of Richard II. (1397). The lordship was later granted
Henry IV. (1400) to Sir John Stanley, Knight, and it continued in his fam
till 41st year of Elizabeth (1599), when William, Earl of Derby, devis

it to Sir William Brereton of Malpas; then it passed into the hands of t
Hanmer and Gwernhaylod families, and during the last quarter of
century the latter portion has since come into the possession of the prese
owner of Bryn-y-pys.

The name Overton has been variously explained. Pennant in l
Tours in North Wales says it is called Ovretone in *Domesday Bc*
(A.D. 1085), which would seem to favour an idea that one, Wlphere,
king of Mercia, in the eighth century, who was a great benefactor to Sax
Churches, might have given his name to the village, *i.e.* Wlpheretc
Especially is this possible, if, as it is said, the original church was of Sax
origin. Again the name Bryn-oovers, commonly called Bryn-hovah, f
the hill between Bangor and Overton, favours this explanation. Anoth
derivation is the simpler, and perhaps therefore the truer, and that is th
Overton is the " Upper town," relative to Bangor-is-y-coed, formerly t
more important place of the two. This also holds to the Saxon origin
the name. While the name Overton is Saxon, its distinctive appellati
of Madoc is certainly British. The reason for its being thus distinguish
is from the existence of another Overton near Malpas in Cheshire. Mad
the son of Meredydd ab Bleddyn, Prince of Powys and Lord of Overtc
is said to have built Overton Castle in the 12th century, and probak
from him came the name Overton Madoc.

Leland (died 1532) in his Itinerary thus mentions this castle. " The
was a praty Pile or Castell at Ovreton yn auncient Tyme, the which w
throuen downe by the violence of Dee river chaunging his Botom. For
olde tyme Dee ran half a mile from the Castel yn a slace of ye vall
caullid Whistan where now is wood and ploughid ground right agai

Ovreton."   And again, " One part of the Diches and Hille of ye Cas
yet remaineth the Resideu is in the Botom of Dee."   There are now
remains of this castle, save perhaps in the tradition that some of the la
stones which were used in the west wall of the churchyard came from so
ruins which stood in what is called Maes y Castell, which is just a li1
below Pen Dyffryn.   The field has been explored without success.   Th
is a wood behind Bryn-y-pys, called Castle Wood, but that name was tl
explained to the writer by Miss Walker of Gwernhaylod.   There wa1
building erected there by some of the Fletchers in which they used to h2
small cannon, and on various occasions these would be fired, but it v
afterwards demolished.   When some men not long ago were digging ab
there, they came upon logs of wood and some masses of brick and mor1
evidently quite modern in their style.   The mystery of the old Ca1
will never be solved, and we must be content with Leland's explanati
that it is the fault of the river Dee.

CHAPTER II.

The District Names of Overton.

IN one of the church papers at Chester, in the deed whic
separated the parishes of Bangor and Worthenbury (bearin
date 1698), these words occur :—" Overton is time out (
mind a parish by itself, consisting of several townships." C
these townships there are now three, viz., Overton Villa
Overton Foreign, and Knolton. Formerly, however, there were six, viz
Higher and Lower Cloy, Higher and Lower Knolton, Maes-y-Lewis, an
Maesguaelod.

The parish embraces an area of 4,095 acres, and a little more, wit
about 275 inhabited houses, and a population in 1831 of *1,796* ; 184:
1,662 ; 1851, *1,479* ; 1861, *1,407* ; 1871, *1,324* ; 1881, *1,125.*

It may be said that roughly the shape of the parish is a square, wit
its four corners—at Overton Bridge, in the Wrexham direction ; at th
White House Cottage, in the direction of Worthenbury ; at the Trottin
Mare Inn, towards Ellesmere ; and at Knolton Mill, looking towarc
Oswestry.

In order to define clearly the bounds of the parish, we look at th
map, and find that on the West the river Dee separates us from Erb
stock ; on the south the little stream called Shellbrook divides Overto
and Dudleston parishes. On the East no very distinct line can be drawi

for a little brook and a number of hedges alone serve to separate th
parish of Penley from our own.   The same may be said of the limits in th
direction of Bangor, that is to say, on the North ; but a line starting fror
the near side of Millbrook Farm and skirting some fields on the crest (
the Brynhovah Hill, across the Bangor Road, down to the Lower Darlan
Plantation by the river, will nearly represent the boundary in that directior

Here perhaps is the best place to point out the spot in the paris
where there is probably the most curious combination of civil and eccles
astical circumstances that can be found anywhere.   On a jutting point (
land below Knolton Hall, where the Shellbrook joins the river, the followin
remarkable conjunction occurs, or did occur till 1849.   One may stand i
England and Wales, in the provinces of Canterbury and York, in th
dioceses of Lichfield, Chester, and St. Asaph ; in the archdeaconries (
Chester, Salop, and St. Asaph ; in the deaneries of Wrexham, Malpa;
and Ellesmere ; in the circuits of Oxford, North Wales, and Chester ; i
the counties of Shropshire, Flintshire, and Denbighshire ; in the hundrec
of Oswestry, Maelor, and Bromfield; in the parishes of Ellesmere, Overtor
and Erbistock ; and in the townships of Dudleston, Knolton, and Erb
stock.   A truly suitable place to elude the officers of the law.

But now to the districts in the parish—their names and explanatior
Following the course of the river, from Overton Bridge downwards, v
come to Asney—spelled also in the parish registers Astney—a meado
land, below the woods of Bryn-y-pys. The meaning of this name is obscur(
The termination *ey* must refer to its having originally been an island ; {
for instance, in the racecourse at Chester, the name Roodeye is the islan
of the rood or cross.   The first syllable *As* (for the *n* is probably put i

for euphony) may be a corruption of the Gaelic *wisg*, which means 'wate
thus Asney would be 'water island'; and this distinctive name would
more appreciated in olden times than now, because there were so many
called islands in the midst of moss and peat districts. The river l
certainly altered its course, and probably flowed round the meadow wh
is now pasture. After leaving Asney we come to the Darland, wh
gives its name to the woods, fields, and plantations around. This na
is clear, it is Torlan (yr afon) the bank (of the river). In the Ordnar
Survey map it is called Darland coch, or red Darland, because of t
colour of the rocks and soil. The landscape here has been much alter
by the landslips in the winter months. From the Darland, across t
fields towards the Bangor road, we enter Bryn-hovah, not a large distri
but a remarkable one; for the name is said to be derived from the fa
that there were the Bryn-hovah gates at or near the crest of the h
overlooking the once celebrated monastery of Bangor Monachorum. Br
means the brow or crest of the hill. Hovah either comes from King O
a king of the Mercians, who drove the Welsh back across the Dee in t
8th century, or Ulphere, another king who obtained possession of t
district of Powysland in the 7th century. "There was also a Hwva
the 12th century, who according to some accounts was steward to Ow
Gwynedd, Prince of North Wales."

Going eastward from Bryn-hovah we come to a district which is cal
Cloy, or The Cloy, which reaches into the parishes of Bangor, Worth
bury, and Penley, and is sub-divided into Upper and Lower Cloy. I ha
come across two derivations for the name; one I found in the late M
Wrench's handwriting, in which he says, " Cloy is a corruption for Cla

I suppose from the clayey nature of the soil." The other explanatio
seems the more probable; it is one given by Pennant. There were tw
gates belonging to the precincts of the Monastery at Bangor, a mile distar
from one another, with the Dee running between them; one was calle
Porth Clais, the other Porth Wgan. The name of the first is retained i
the name of Cloy, and the second in the name of a house called Hogar
This name has also been found " Llai," thus recalling the Welsh or ancier
British name of the place.

Leaving Cloy, and walking towards Ellesmere, we come to that lon
stretch of common-land called Lightwood Green. Two parishes hav
an interest in this district, Penley and Overton, for the two parishes joi
halfway across the Green. This name is Saxon, deriving itself from th
" laed," which means a division of a county; it is written Laith-wood i
the Penley map. It is a fact that the boundary line between Flintshir
and Shropshire, and between two ancient parishes, does actually run her
and therefore there may be a likelihood of this derivation being the righ
one. Thus it would stand somewhat thus, the " Green of the wood whic
forms the boundary."

From Lightwood Green, keeping on the outskirts of the parish, w
come to Knolton Bryn and Knolton. The Bryn is only a part of th
township or district of Knolton. It is not difficult to find an explanatio
for this name. It is the town or hamlet of the knolls, or little hills, an
that is just the description of the place. From Llan-y-Cefn toward
Dudleston and Ellesmere there are a succession of knolls, and the highes
ground in the parish is in a farm above the new house called Bryn Tirior

Continuing westward we come to the Gwalliau. It is a Welsh nam€

.as its termination *au* shows; the ending denotes the plural numb
There are in fact two Gwallias, and around these two farms lies the disti
which receives its designation from them. Gwallia is the Brito-Rom
name for Wales. Gwall is the Welsh for a wall, or for any land enclosed
.a wall. Possibly it may have reference to the Castle which was near,
simply to its being on the borders of Shropshire and Flintshire, where
.a wall of division, and this part of Wales is, I am told, called Cyn
·Gwallia. Another district is the Trench, in which this parish has only
little interest. It seems to take its name from that deep little valley tl
·runs all the way from Dudleston to Bangor, which may have formed so
boundary line centuries ago.
    Our last district, which is almost in the centre of the parish is Argo
Ar means in Welsh, above; goed or coed has the meaning of a wo
This describes the position of the district. But at the same time there
.something further to be learnt. In other places where the name occurs
" seems to be the name of the camps made by the Britons by felling
wood and heeping them up, as is done in all woody countries to this da·
It is to be remembered that the monks of Bangor were a distinctly warl
body, as may been seen from the way in which they resisted the invas:
·of their domains in the early history of Christianity. There may ha
been a camp near Argoed. There certainly is a large mound or tumu
behind Gwernhaylod and near Brynypys, but that is probably a mod·
·contention going by the name of the Giant's Grave. The late M
Walker used to say there was a legend that it was there that the Gi;
Althrey in fear of his enemies died, having taken the great stride fr·
Bangor to Overton.

BRYN-Y-PYS.

CHAPTER III.

Ube Ibouse IRames of Overton.

TURNING from the districts to the names of the houses i
neighbourhood of Overton, omitting those which are ob
in their meaning, I propose to take the larger ones
noticing also one or two that have disappeared. Sta
from Overton Bridge, one of the first houses that would
met the eye, would have been Maesgwaelod, owned by the Hanmer
Fletchers. In this house, I believe, the late Lord Hanmer and the pr
Sir W. E. Hanmer were born, and by a Mrs. Elizabeth Hanmer o
same house, was given the Church plate. The house subsequ
became the home of Major Fletcher, one of the Gwernhaylod family
commanded the rear of the British army at the battle of Corunna, in
On leaving the city, he took away the keys of the gates, and for some
they hung at Maesgwaelod, held together by a steel plate, bearing tl
scription " Portigo de Puerta de Abigo." " Maesgwaelod " is " Lower f
a name derived from the position it occupied. It has given its title t
little district which surrounded the house. Above Maesgwaelod, t

north, stands Bryn-y-pys, part of which was built in the year 1739; b
the house has been so much altered at different times, that little of tl
very old part still remains.   The house once belonged to the Prices, ar
now it is owned—and long may it continue to be owned—by E. Peel, Es
The meaning of the name given by some is the " Brow of the Pea-field
taken from some field existing long ago.   Others explain it as " Brow
the Cross," " Brow of the Magpies," or " Brow of the Promontory;" tl
meaning, perhaps, is immaterial.   Near this house, on a rising grour
opposite, was the Cayah, or Caeau (The Fields), formerly inhabited l
Colonel Fletcher, but this house has been pulled down some time.   North
Bryn-y-pys, overlooking the valley of the Dee, commanding a view unsu
passed in the neighbourhood, stands Gwernhaelyd, or Gwernhaylod.   Tl
house itself was probably rebuilt in the beginning of the last century; i
any rate, the Fletchers seem to have come into the neighbourhood abor
that time.   In another chapter the pedigree is touched on; this fami
was perhaps the oldest and best established in the parish, tracing bac
their descent as far as the Princes of North Wales.   Gwern means mars
or swamp; haylod, probably means sunny, for heulog or haulog (pr(
nounced hailog) in the Welsh; so that the house derives its name fro
the land below, which may have been really at one time, a " sunny marsh
" This house was the abode of Badi, alias Madoc ap Howel, in the time
Edward IV.   He rebuilt the house, and from about 1460 to 1490 l
flourished there."   This is an extract from the Salusbury Pedigree in tl
Hengwrt and Caerwys MSS.
       We must pass through the village to find another name to fathor
and the name " Llan-y-Cefn " attracts the ear; referring probably

Erbistock Church.   Llan is a sacred enclosure, and Erbistock Ch
and churchyard is the only thing of the kind near that can be so descri
Passing on to some other names of places in the village, we have t
Pens : " Pen-y-bryn," " Pen-y-llan," and " Pendas." The first two
self-evident.   Pen-y-bryn, from its position, means the " head of
brow."   Pen-y-llan also indicates the locality of the houses which
the name, " The head of the village," for Llan, besides meaning a sa
enclosure, gives its name to any place where there is or has been a chu
and, as almost every village has a church, it comes to mean the villag
village street itself.   But Pendas puzzles me.   It has been sugge
that a corruption has taken place, and that once the word was Pen-y
" the head of the town," and that the two ends of the village were di
guished as Pen-y-llan and Pen-y-dre.   This may be so.   Proba
however, Pendas is really Pentice or Penthouse, pointing out the shap
the building, which was a " lean-to," used for the Magistrates' Court.
Chester, the magistrates' court had of old the same name, derived :
the building in which it was held.   It was this fact that gave the h
the designation of Town Hall.   The house which stands on the c
side of the street is called the " Quinta;" this word probably is Spar
meaning a " cottage."   Why or how it got its name it is impossibl
say; because, though Overton has English and Welsh names, it is stra
that any other language should find its way here, and this explana
may be derived from the fact that the house called the Quinta,
Chirk, received the title from being *five* (quinque) miles from Oswes
possibly our Quinta is so called because it is five miles from Ruabon.
Going out of the village towards Bangor, the strangest name in

parish appears, " Carigo-france " farm, sometimes also spelled Carreg-y-francis.   It is certainly hard to find out a derivation for this word.   Now it is clear that the first two syllables, carig or carreg, are from the Welsh word cerrig or carreg, which means a " heap of stones," or merely "stones," but stones of what ?   One suggests France has to do with some Frankish settlers in years gone by, who also settled at Frankton and had a trade, which failed, and so they disappeared; he calls to his help the Tre-y-peni or Dre-y-peni, wood, because peni has, like the first syllable of Penley, and the second part of the name of the house in Penley parish called Llanerch Panna, the signification of a " fuller " or cleaner of cloth which trade the Frankish settlers were engaged in.   But the second derivation is more likely, I think, and this points to the word " Ffrangcon," a beaver, and thus suggests that Carreg-y-ffrangcon is the " stones of the beaver."   There is a well-known valley in Carnarvonshire, called Nant francon," the valley of the beavers."   The beaver has long ago left Britain but the name still remains for any water animal, perhaps the otter.

We will consider three other names before we pass to the other side of the parish; one is " Cae Dyah," probably Cae Dafid, " David's Field "; for I am told that Dafid the Welsh saint has had his name changed into wondrously many forms, and it is right that we should claim an interest in him.

On the outskirts of the parish is " Pant Poulton " farm.   Pant or Pont is the Welsh for a bridge, so that probably the bridge below the farm gives it its name; perhaps a man named Poulton built it.   Just off the Upper Cloy-lane is the " Nant " farm, which overlooks the deep ravine which runs through what are called the Duke's woods on to

Bangor, and receives its designation from it; for Nant is the V
for a valley or a ravine.

Continuing our journey over the parish, we come across the
called Plas-yn-y-coed, " the house in the wood," which fairly
describes its position. One of the prettiest walks in the neighbou1
is through the fields belonging to this farm, across the brook a
bottom, and through the woods into the Cloy. Not far from this
near Little Overton, is the " Tan House farm." This receives its
from the fact that some years ago there was a tanyard here; the pi
remains in which the skins in the raw state were dipped before being ta1
There is a date in the wall of the house, on a black stone inserted a
the doorway, with the name of the builder, " Tho Langford Struxi1
Dom. 1772." The architecture is much the same externally a:
majority of the houses in the village. This farm gives its name
row of cottages which belonged to the farm—Tan House Row.

At the bottom of the hill, off the road leading to Penley, i:
" Canister " Hall, a name given to the four cottages, well known a
Watkin's Cottages, which join one another with one central chin
the whole building having a strong resemblance to a tea canister.
the lane which runs past the gas-house, and on to Lightwood G
stand two farms, " Mussley " and " Lightwood Hall." The forme1
strange names. One wonders whether it is a mixture of English
Welsh—Maes, a field, and ley, a field—or whether it is a corrupti(
the name Maes Lewis, Lewis's field, or part of Lewis's land, fo
district beyond, towards the Trotting Mare, is all distinguished by
name. I incline to the second derivation.

Lightwood Hall has the same origin as Lightwood Green. It w
a house well known in the past, for a branch of the Pulestons of Emr
and Worthenbury lived there as far back as 1615. It is now owned I
Sir Watkin Williams Wynn.   We turn back to the Ellesmere roa
On the left hand side of the road is "Queen's bridge" farm, taking i
name from the bridge over a little brook a few yards farther on. I a
told that the name Queen's bridge is due to Queen Eleanor, who we
this way to Carnarvon Castle, where the first Prince of Wales was bor
This is the tradition.   Probably no one can vouch for its correctnes
During the repairs done some little time ago to the structure of tl
bridge, the following inscription was discovered on a stone in the wa
"This bridge was repaired 1626. Thomas Lloyd, gent., and Rog
Edwards, overseers."

Just a little farther on the road is the farm which is called "Ma
Lewis" now, but originally called "Crab Mill."   Here we have
remnant of an ancient industry.   Crab apples used to be crushed he
to make verjuice, which was supposed to be an excellent remedy f
bruises and wounds.   The mill has disappeared; probably the nan
will not.

We now turn to the right past Bryntirion, over Knolton Bryn, ar
where four roads meet we find the "Rhewl" farm.   Rhewl, I understan
means road; and I suppose is so called because it is the farm by tl
cross roads.   Near Gobowen is a little hamlet called the Rhewl.   Goir
further still to the extreme boundaries of the parish, there used to stand
farm—now only a shed for cattle—called the "Caeau," the fields,
common name it seems, but now only remaining in memory for tv

houses at each end of the parish which have disappeared. The l
house in the parish in this direction is the Knolton Mill—Barto
Mill as it used to be called; as it stands now, it was built in 1760,
the present building replaced an older one farther down the Shellbro
built, I believe, by Roger Barton, of Knolton Hall, who died about 16

Chapter IV.

The Municipal—Parliamentary—History of Overton.

IN the first chapter we gave a derivation for Overton as
"upper town"; it is of the latter term, as applied
the village, that we write now. Overton is a borough
very important place in its way. We are accustomed
speak of the village as the town, as opposed to the dist
which we called the country, and rightly so, for it has had one mayo
not more than one. No corporation ever existed apparently, but a ma
was once elected, and for the matter of that, an alderman too. In
year 1830, the Market Hall, which stands in High Street was built,
which markets and fairs were held (according to the inscription which s
remains) for one or two years, the fairs days being April 21st, August 2
and October 8th; the markets, every Saturday at 12 o'clock. To celebr
this occasion one William Edge of Pen-y-llan was chosen mayor
Overton, but he died not long after his appointment. It is said he w
succeeded by one Alderman Phillips of Carigo France farm, but we
inclined to think the title and dignity died with the first mayor, for marke
fairs, and mayor appear to have disappeared at the same time. There w

mayors of the Green,* who were possibly presidents of the old Frienc
Society of Overton, which had its meetings at the Bowling Green Ir
Besides these, there do not seem to have been any other mayors, thou
I have been told the house at the end of the village used to be called t
Town Hall, but that was because it was the place of meeting of magistrat

In February, 1880, a commission was appointed to look into t
state of the municipal corporations of various places, and it is said tł
"the report 1835 is supposed to be correct except that it mentions as
"charter" what is really only a grant of a market, and omits the otł
charter granted 13 years after. This one, which has since been discovei
at the †Public Record Office, provides among other things that Overt
should be a free borough, that the burgesses were to elect 300 uprig
men as bailiffs, and that the king's bailiff of Maelor Hundred was to sel
one of them as bailiff of the town. The report adds, there are no bail;
or other officers, no municipality of judicial ground, and no property. T
magistrates for the county grant licenses to public houses."

But now we come to a more important part of the Borough histo
namely its Parliamentary nature. Overton is one of those places whi
unite, under the title of the Flint Boroughs, in sending a member
Parliament. A brief history of the boroughs may be interesting. In 15
Flint received by itself the right of a borough, of electing a Member
Parliament, and its first representative was " Edward Stanley de Fly

*See Chapter vii.
†Charter Rolls, 7 Ed. I., No. 23 (Overton market and fair), 20 Ed. I., No. 55. (Over
Burgh).

armiger." It continued in solitude till 1685, when Flint, Rhyddla
Caerwys, Alcen, and Caergwrle, were joined together, under the title
the Flint Boroughs.   The member then elected was a Sir John Hanme
This state of things continued till 1702, when, according to the Parlia
mentary Register, issued in the *Blue Book* 1880, the boroughs were Flin
Rhyddlan, Overton, Caerwys, and Caergwrle.   The first member of th
boroughs thus constituted, was Sir John Conway.   The M.P.'s, till 183
were the following :—1702, Sir John Conway ; 1702, Sir. Roger Mostyn
1702, Thomas Mostyn ; 1705, Sir Roger Mostyn (again) ; 1708, Sir Joh
Conway (again) ; 1713, Sir Roger Mostyn (third time) ; 1721, Thoma
Eyton ; 1721, Salusbury Lloyd ; 1734, Sir George Wynne ; 1741, Richar
Williams ; 1747, Kyffn Williams ; 1761, Sir John Glynne ; 1777, Watki
Williams (Constable of Flint Castle) ; 1806, Sir E. Pryce Lloyd ; 180
William Shipley ; 1817, Sir E. Pryce Lloyd (again, afterwards title
Lord Mostyn) ; 1831, Henry Glynne.   After the passing of the Refor
Act, 1832, the Flint Boroughs were as follows, and have continued so ti
now, viz. :—Flint, Rhyddlan, Overton, Caerwys, Caergwrle, St. Asapl
Holywell, and Mold.   The M.P.'s from 1832 have been : 1832 and 183
Sir R. Glynne ; 1837, Charles Whalley Dean Dundas ; 1841, Sir Richar
Bulkeley Williams Bulkeley ; 1847, Sir John Hanmer ; 1868, Sir Robe
Alfred Cunliffe ; 1872, Peter Ellis Eyton ; 1878, John Roberts, who was r
elected in 1880.   This is not a place to discuss politics, but according t
returns in the whole boroughs, party feeling represented pretty regularl
only one side of the House of Commons.   It may be well at this point to ad
the names of those who have served as High Sheriffs of Flintshire fro
Overton parish.   The first apparently was Thomas Lloyd, in 1650.   In 166

John Wynne of Overton.   1670, Owen Wynne of Overton.   1675, O
Barton of Knolton.   1690, Thomas Lloyd of Gwernhaylod.   1695, J
Wynne of Overton.   1697, Owen Barton of Knolton.   1727, Maurice Wy
of Plasynycoed.   1737, Francis Price of Brynypys.   1755, John Barke
Overton.   1764, Richard Parry Price of Brynypys.   1767, Philip Ll
Fletcher of Gwernhaylod.   1774, Owen Wynne of Overton.   1803, O
Molyneux Wynne of Overton.   1810, Francis Richard Price of Bryny
1870, Edmund Peel of Brynypys.

THE CEMETERY.

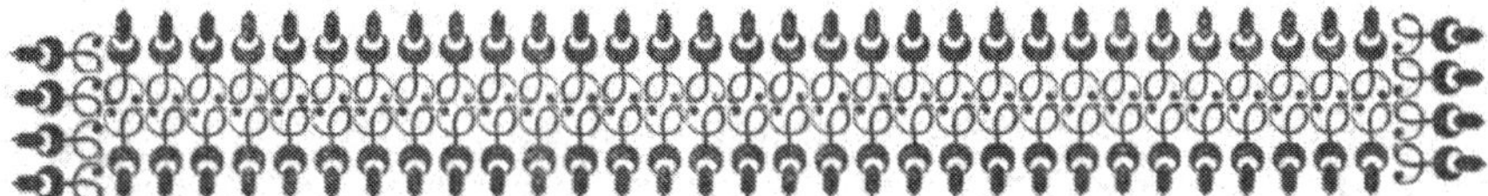

Chapter V.

The Church of Overton.

THE church dedicated to Mary the Mother of our Lord nc shall occupy our attention; and well worthy it is of notic for it is one of the prettiest churches in the neighbourhoo Of course it cannot compare with Holt, or Hanmer, Gresford, which are remarkable in very many points; yet f all that, it may compare favourably with most of those in the villag round.

As has been mentioned, it is traditionally supposed to occupy the si of an ancient Saxon church, which possessed a beacon on the top of tl tower for signalling to the neighbourhood whenever an invasion was appr hended. But whatever there was, nothing now remains of Saxon dat unless we except a curious stone which was discovered some years a{ in the east wall of the churchyard. Mr. Bloxam, an antiquary great eminence, pronounced it to be Saxon. There is upon it representation of a figure, half length; the two hands are fold together over the heart. It has probably been the top of a sto

coffin.   Near it was found another stone also used in the buildi[ng]
of the wall with some rude lettering carved upon it, apparently of t[he]
same date, but there is considerable difficulty in deciphering any [of]
the letters.

Canon Thomas, in his *History of the Diocese of St. Asaph*, th[us]
describes the exterior:—"The church, St. Mary's, consists of chanc[el]
nave, with north and south aisles, and a western tower, the gene[ral]
character being perpendicular, i.e., about 1450-1500, but with o[ne]
or two features of earlier pointed work."   Lewis, in his *Encyclopæd[ia]*
says the style is Early English, and that "the tower whi[ch]
appears to be of later date is supposed to have been built wh[en]
the church was reduced in dimension by the removal of the transe[pt]
and the original tower at the intersection which had fallen in[to]
decay."

It is difficult to harmonise these two accounts, and from all appe[ar]
ances the work was throughout of perpendicular style, and apparen[tly]
consisted originally of nave and a north transept chapel, with p[os]
sibly a south aisle.   "The tower externally," once more to qu[ote]
Canon Thomas, "is a fine feature, having buttresses and battlemen[ts]
with a polygonal turret rising above its north-east angle."   (T[his]
feature is singularly unique in this district; it is more like the tow[er]
of some of the churches in the weald of Kent).   On the east fa[ce]
of the tower there are two strange-faced gargoyles, and they are t[he]
only things of the kind in the church.   On the same side is [a]
moulding string course, showing the original height of the na[ve]
roof.

The chancel was added in 1710, the north aisle in 1819, and th
south aisle, the gift of the late Misses Bennion, in 1855.

On the south wall of the tower, just over the vestry, is a sun-dial, pι
up in 1803. The words above the dial are "Carpe Diem," below it, "Si
Vita," and the words, "Our days upon earth are a shadow."—Job viii., 9
then underneath are the names of the Churchwardens, J. Hughes an
W. Clay, and the names of the designer, John Baines, and the sculptoι
George Broadbent. The inscriptions on sundials are always instructive.

Entering the church by the west door in the tower, it is to be notice
that the floor of the ringing chamber has been altered; it formerly cam
half-way down the west window of the tower, but at the restoration in 187ζ
it was raised, and the ropes carried down to the floor. The clock work
now stand in the chamber, which originally was the ringers' chamber. Th
new clock was put into the church, and the quarter chimes arranged i
December, 1862, the money being raised by public subscription. Abov
the clock chamber is the belfry, where there is a peal of six bells. Th
tenor bell is the oldest (there originally being two bells and a cracked one
and bears this inscription : " 1615, Gloria Deo in Excelsis " (Glory to Go
in the highest). The other five were hung in the year 1826, and hav
these words : " E. Lowe, Churchwarden, John Rudhead, fecit." Th
windows, which are much dilapidated, and which, it is hoped, ere lon
may be restored, have very pretty tracery; the north one was broke
to pieces by one of the bells getting loose in ringing, and bounding oι
into the churchyard. A fine view of the surrounding country may b
obtained from the corner turret; on a fine day Chester Cathedral an
Town Hall can easily be seen.

Descending to the ground floor, notice should be taken of the mode
vestry room, which was built in the year 1819. The old vestry was on 1
ground floor of the tower, and the present entrance was a fireplace, 1
tower originally being entered by an outside door. Inside the room :
one or two things to be mentioned ; the first being the old parish che
which has evidently been made from one huge trunk. The lock is
magnificent old piece of ironwork ; within the chest are a few old boo
and some papers of recent date, though a few documents date as far b;
as 1639, but they are merely indentures of apprenticeship, agreements, a
bills. There are also two old brass candlesticks which have a histc
The inscription is this : " Margeret Eyton, spinster, daughter of Thon
Eyton, gent., and Elioner his wife, her guift to ye Parish Church of Ov
ton Maddock in Com : Flint to put every Christmas Day with burn
candles in them in ye morning before day on ye graves of the said Thor
Eyton and Elioner his wife, and Thophilus their son." The candlesti
were lost or hidden away since the restoration of the church, but h;
been found and given back for the use of the vestry. The registers are k
in a safe in the wall. The old font also stands here. The first time it v
used was in 1747, the registers having the following : " 1747, 1st cl
baptised in new marble font in Freeholder's Chancell, the gift of Frar
Price, Esq., of Bryn-y-pece," (sic). The registers are not very early,
it is possible to find registers going back as far 1557 ; for the great m
date for keeping registers of baptisms, marriages, and burials in e;
parish was issued in 1538. This mandate was repeated in more rigor
terms in 1558, but as it was not sufficiently attended to, it was ordai;
in 1597 that parchment books should be purchased at the expense of e

parish.   The baptism register has the earliest entry, namely, 1601, t
come the burials 1602, and the marriages 1603.   There are breaks in
continuity of them, sometimes of thirteen years.   There are very
remarks besides the entry of the names.   They are as a rule not signe{
anyone, but only occasionally at the end of a quarter.   In 1778 there is
death recorded of " Margaret the Harper."   It is supposed she was {
nected with the well-known harpist, who lived near Overton Bridge.
the old register, Bryn-y-pys is almost invariably spelled Bryn-a-p
The oldest are carefully bound together, and safely kept in a box by th
selves.   Some of the writing is beautifully and carefully done.

    When anyone formerly entered the church from the west door,
would pass under a gallery supported on wooden columns, wherein at
time stood the organ and the choir.   For at that time the church was
seated as it is now, but the old-fashioned square pews, each of wl
accommodated a whole family, filled the church from end to end.   {
gallery came half-way down the east arch of the tower, and hid wh{
now open to view.   The organ was moved from the gallery to the {
end of the north aisle, where it stood till the restoration, when the
one, built in 1854, was removed to the east end of the same aisle.
that time the east window of the wall, apparently from what remains {
in a garden near the village, was rather a fair specimen of the deb{
English style, *i.e.* about 1500, but it was removed, and a small addition
way of an organ chamber, now used as a vestry, was made by contin{
the aisle eastward.   As has been said, the north and south aisles {
added during this century, the nave thus being the only old part of
church.   The roof was with an arched lath and plaster ceiling, low,

therefore the alteration, after restoration, must have been most noticeabl
in the dealing with that; for now the clerestory windows, in what is calle
a handsome beam roof, supported on pilasters of stone, strike the ey
directly one enters the church.   At the base of one of the western pillar:
there is worked into the last stone what apparently was an early coffi
lid, on which there is a cross carved.   At the west end of the south aisl
stands the new font; the inscription says : "This font was given to Overto
Church by the tenants and friends of E. Peel, Esq., to commemorate th
christening of his son, Hugh Edmund Ethelston Peel, Feb 1st, A.D. 1872.
The design is to illustrate the two types of baptism, the crossing the Re
Sea and the Ark, and the baptism of our Lord and His blessing littl
children.   In the south aisle the east and south-east windows are fille
with stained glass; the east one to the memory of Dorothea Bennion, wh
died 1852, and the other to Caroline Bennion, who died 1847.

We now enter the chancel to examine what there is for noting dow
First of all let it be borne in mind that the chancel proper was built i
1710.   A stone that used to be over the east window before the restoratio
had upon it that date.   The restoration was undertaken in 1870 by th
Rector, the Rev. H. Mackenzie, through the liberality of Edmund Pee
Esq., of Bryn-y-pys, to whose generosity the final restoration of the whol
church is almost entirely due.   The floor was raised and the roof als
while the seating and windows were altered.   It is said that upon the do
of the pew on the north side, which was at one time occupied by a famil
from Ellesmere, named Kynaston, who lived some few years at Knolto
Hall, were the words "Protectoris auctoritate, 1649." The words wer
to commemorate the fact that Oliver Cromwell stayed a night at Knolto

Of course that pew could not have been the identical one which
Protector sat in, as the dates will indicate, but Overton should be pi
of having been even a stopping-place of Oliver Cromwell. (?)   The wind
of the chancel are well worth examining.   They are all three by
same artists, Clayton and Bell.   The east window was placed in
church by E. Peel, Esq., in 1869.   The north window was put up in men
of Thomas Lloyd Fletcher and Charlotte his wife, who died respecti
in 1830 and 1839.   The south window has the following inscription (
brass plate on the window sill, " In memory of John ap Ellis E;
upwards of 40 years surgeon in the parish of Overton, who died Sept.
1865, aged 69 years.   This window was erected by public subscriptior
a mark of the high esteem in which he was held by all classes."

Before turning to the monuments and tablets in the church, men
should be made of the beautiful Communion plate.   It is silver gilt,
the inscription on the two plates and chalices as well as on the fla
is:—" Overton Chappel Plate, exchanged by the desire and at the exp(
of Mrs. Elizabeth Hanmer, of Maesguaylod, 1783."   There is beside
little plate of earlier date, probably 1740, perhaps belonging to the old
for which the present was exchanged.   One other thing deserves no:
and that is the old brass candelabra of twelve lights, which hangs {
the middle of the roof of the chancel; a dove hovers over the lights, ty}
of the Holy Spirit, and the words on the body of the work are :—"
gift of Cath. Humphries, widow, 1746."

The tablets and ornaments in the church shall now occupy our at
tion, and in passing a remark may be made about the duty of preser
all ancient monuments which has been neglected in the past.   It is

that for instance in the vestry were two old monuments which have bee
taken away and an interesting connecting link with the past has thus bee
destroyed. The brass tablets, too, were well nigh eaten away with rus
The best system to follow will be to take the different families who hav
put up monuments to their friends, and in this a beginning shall be mad
with the Lloyds, of Halghton. A brass tablet hidden away but no
placed on the eastern wall of the nave, has this inscription :—" M. S
Ursulæ Lloyd uxoris Tho. Lloyd de Halghton in Parochæ de Hanme
armigeri Sepultæ Maii 24, 1664. Tho. Lloyd de Halghton armige
sepulti Sept. 30, 1693, Æt. 73." Two children of this Thomas Lloyd an
Ursula his wife have mention made of them in the church. One has
tablet to herself, which is hidden away behind the organ, and as she wa
a benefactor to the parish of £20 (a good deal in those days), it seems
pity that her memorial should be lost to view. The inscription is : " I
memory of Mrs. Beatrice Lloyd, second daughter of Thomas Lloyd,
Halghton, Esq., by Ursula Conway, of Portryddis, who discharged all
her duties relating to this life, and the good works and alms-deed
honoured and lamented by all. She departed this life the 2nd Decembe
A.D. 1708.

The other child is a son, who is mentioned in the large monument i
Latin on the north side of the east window, the original and translatio
of which would take up too much space, so only the translation is given

" Sacred to the memory of Mary, the daughter and heiress of Willia
Phillips, Esq., of Gwernhayled, and Anna, his wife. She married Thoma
the youngest child of Thomas Lloyd, Esq., of Halghton. She was
faithful and most affectionate wife to him ; a dutiful mother to her childre

for whose welfare she was always anxious. In all the duties of life, sh
was in the highest degree worthy the imitation of wives. She died th
14th March, 1728, aged 67 years. Also to the loved memory of Thoma:
their only son, who took as the dear partner of his life, Alice, the daughte
of John Cleveland, Esq., of Liverpool, by whom he had an only daughtei
who survived him. While he lived, he was a kind and indulgent husbanc
and a true friend, upright and firm to his purpose in all things ; as he wa
when alive, the joy of friends and their families, so when he died, he le
such regret amongst all, that his survivors thought it a wrong thing tha
their and the country's tears and loss should not be borne witness to i
this monument. He died July 12th, 1730, aged 32 years. Also i
memory of Anne, the only child of Thomas and Alice Lloyd, a favourit
with all, who died Dec. 8th, 1734, aged 7 years."

We find on the north side, within the rails, one of the oldest monument
of the time of Queen Anne. There is a considerable amount of gilding, bu
the work is principally confined to heads of cherubs. The inscription is :—
"Underneath lies the body of Edward Phillips of Gwernhaylod, in th
county of Flint, Esq., who married Mary, daughter and co-heir to Thoma
Overton of Overton, Esq., he died the 23rd of April, A.D. 1681. Her
also lyeth the body of William, son and heir to the said Edward Phillips
Esq., and Mary his wife, who died the 30th of August, A.D. 1688. He lei
issue 4 daughters by Anne his wife, eldest daughter of Captain Williar
Broughton, son of Morgan Broughton of Marchwiel, in the county c
Denbigh, Esq. She (being also here interred) departed this life the 12t
of March, A.D. 1705-6. Mrs. Katherine Phillips, daughter of the sai
William Phillips, by Anne his wife, as a testimony of her affectio

to so near and dear relations, erected this monument to their memor
A.D. 1713."

The interest of this monument consists in the fact that it states tha
there was a family Overton of Overton; it will be interesting to trace th
pedigree hereafter.　Three names are here commemorated, which deser
our gratitude.　One Mrs. Phillips (I suppose Anne Phillips) gave £5 fc
the poor; a second, Captain William Broughton, gave £5 also; and th
third, Mrs. Katherine Phillips, gave £10, as witnesses the board c
charities in the vestry.　Another point to be noticed is the connectio
with the Lloyds of Halghton.　The eldest daughter of William Phillip
(Mary) married the second Thomas Lloyd of Halghton.　It is throug
this name Phillips that Gwernhaylod has come into the hands of th
Fletchers, so that in the monument on the south of the east window w
have the three names in Phillips Lloyd Fletcher, who died Nov. 26tl
1808, and is described thus:—" He was a most affectionate husbanc
brother, father.　He did justice, loved mercy, and walked humbly wit
his God.　He was in death a Christian, as in life a friend."　From thi
last monument we find the connection with a great family also commemc
rated in the chancel, namely the Wynnes of Gwydir.　This Phillip
Lloyd Fletcher married Eleanor, the daughter of Owen Wynne of Llwyr
who died 30th August, 1780, and to his memory a monument was erecte
in the south side of the chancel by his second wife, a daughter c
Broughton Whitehall, Esq. of Broughton, and he is described as "
tender and indulgent husband, an affectionate parent, a kind master,
sincere friend, and a honest man."　His son (a brother of the abov
Eleanor Wynne), Maurice Wynne, LL.D., according to the tablet nex

The Church of Overton.

to the above, was thirty-six years Rector of Bangor-cum-Overton, and
"last male descendant of the house of Gwydir." He died in May, 1
We are now almost at the end of these reminiscences. There
two or three monuments yet to be noticed in the church, belongin;
names known and respected in the past. For instance, in the chancel
on the north aisle are tablets put up to the memory of the Price;
Bryn-y-pys. The earliest date is that of Francis Price, a son of Cap
Richard Price of "Bryn-y-peice." He died in 1749. He "planned
conduct of his life by that noble comprehensive rule—to do justice, l
mercy, and walk humbly with God in the conscientious discharge of
several duties of a husband, a parent, a magistrate, a master, a fri∈
and a neighbour; lived, beloved, and died generally lamented." His ;
Francis Parry Price, died in 1787, "a most indulgent and affectior
husband"; this monument is within the communion rails. Fra;
Richard Price, the last of the family, who died in 1858, was the latt
only son. His second wife, Eliza Partridge Price, bequeathed s∈
money for the Clothing Club in Overton.
Then there is a tablet to the memory of Roger Barton of Knol
Hall, a number of whose kindred are recorded in the registers. A b;
tablet to "John Eyton, gent., grandson of Sir Robert Eyton of Pen
madock."* The date is 1734. Two mural tablets in the chancel to
memory of Thomas Hanmer, Roger Hanmer, John Hanmer, and N
Mary Hanmer of Maesguaylod, "the last remaining branches of a fan

*Sir Robert Eyton of Pentref-madoc was taken prisoner with Sir Gerard Eyton (
1653) of Eyton, Knight, banneret, by the Parliamentary troops under Colonel Myttoi
Eyton.

long resident and much respected in this neighbourhood." The date
vary from 1730 to 1794. A sister of these brothers gave the church plate
Three tablets are connected with Llan-y-cefn, one in memory of Joh
Edwards, Esq., 1769; one to Rev. Edward Meeson, 1821; and anothe
of the same name, 1848. There is a monument to Thomas Bennion, th
father of the three munificent sisters, Dorothea, Caroline, and Mary An
Bennion of Wrexham-fechan. Mrs. Walker of Gwernhayled, Kendric
Price (1790), John Wynne Fletcher, Colonel Jones of Knolton, Matthe
Gostling, Esq. (1783), are also commemorated by tablets to their names.
And now for some words about our lovely Cemetery. This wa
opened and consecrated on June 17th, 1872, as well as the chapel; afte
a long and arduous work to complete the drainage and the building of th
wall; it was then handed over to the parish by Edmund Peel, Esq.; th
parishioners gratefully welcoming the gift, which is now amongst th
wonders and beauties of North Wales. The windows in the chapel ar
beautiful: six little ones depict "The Nativity," "The Baptism in th
River Jordan," "The Rising of Jairus's Daughter," "The Angel at th
Sepulchre," "The Ascension," "The Raising of Lazarus." The wes
window has for its subject: "The Heavenly Choir of Angels." The eas
window: "The Good Shepherd," "Christ in Glory," and "Christ Bearin
the Cross." These windows are all the design of O'Connor, a well-know
artist in stained glass. The chapel was built by Mr. W. M. Teulon
who also was entrusted with the restoration of the church. The cemeter
should be anxiously and lovingly guarded by the parishioners of Overton
Lastly we come to the names of the Clergy who have ministered i
Overton, at any rate, since it belonged to the diocese of Chester and St

Asaph.   For be it remembered, we have passed through many changes ⟨
Bishops.   First of all, Overton was in Lichfield and Coventry, then i
Chester, now in St. Asaph.   The separation of Chester from Lichfiel
and Coventry took place in 1541.   There is no mention of Overton :
the episcopal books of Lichfield, and in Exton's "Thesaurus" the followir
is found, "Overton alias Orton-Madoc S. Mary Capella (in Bangor Parisl
co. Flint nothing perpetual certified," so that all we can discover is 1
be found at Chester.   Within a very few years Overton has changed Rur
Deans, being first in Malpas, then in Wrexham, and now in Bangor-is-
Coed Rural Deanery; so it is difficult to get an exact list of the clerg
Formerly, therefore, Overton was a curacy under the Rectors of Bango
In 1630, Evan Jones was curate; 1674, Michael Jones; 1685, Jam(
Owens; 1718, Andrew Lloyd (he was buried in Overton Churchyard
1722, John Jennings; 1739, Samuel Roe; 1745, Joshua Adams; 176
Zacchæus Ellis; 1796, Frederick Lloyd; 1806, Joseph Venables; 181
Lloyd Fletcher; 1836, Henry Knapp; 1841, Harry Ovenden Wrencl
1859, Thomas Douglas.   In 1868, on the death of the late Rector
Bangor-is-y-coed, Overton was separated from Bangor, and became
Rectory in the patronage of His Grace the Duke of Westminster, K.C
whose father, the late Marquis of Westminster, had bought the advows(
from the Gwernhaylod family.   The first Rector was Henry Mackenzi
1868; the second, George John Howson, 1879.

Chapter VI.

The Charities of Overton.

I T is proposed to give in this chapter some accounts of th[e] Parochial Charaties, and first, of that charity connected wit[h] St. Thomas's Day, commonly called the Flannel Charity. [It] is due almost entirely to the exertions and investigations [of] the late Rev. H. O. Wrench, and the late Mr. C. E. Studle[y] that we know what we do of this matter. It is as likely as not, that, ha[d] they not kept a careful look-out, this charity might have disappeared, an[d] been lost to the parish. The following is some account of its history, [as] gleaned from the board in the vestry, dated 1750, when Rev. Joshua Adam[s] was curate-in-charge, and John Ellice and William Powell were churc[h] wardens.

Some land in the parish of Overton, bordering on the Queen[s] bridge, Lightwood Hall, and Crab Hill Farms, called Maes-y-Barty[,] containing nine acres and twenty-five perches, was bequeathed [to] "the Poor of the Chapelry of Overton," by one "John Lloyd[,] date and residence unknown. The trustees are "the Minister an[d] Overseers." There is no deed in existence to restrict the trustees as [to]

the disposal of the yearly rent of this land, and it would therefore appea
that the application of it is left to their own discretion.   The rent is no\
£7 per annum.   Until the year 1877, £4 was annually paid by the overseer
of the parish to the trustees of the Maes-y-Bartys land, being the interes
on £80, and is thus accounted for.   About the year 1810, some timbe
growing on the said land was cut down and sold; part of the produce wa
spent in replanting the land, and the surplus, £80, was paid to Mr. F. R
Price, in part discharge of a sum of £360 lent by him to the parish for th
purpose of building the Poorhouse on Lightwood Green.   When the com
mon land was taken in in 1878, the sum of £3 was paid to the trustees a
the allotment connected with the Maes-y-Bartys land.

The land in Penley, containing nine acres, three roods and ten perches
was bought in the year 1732, and the purchase-money was made up c
certain sums that had been previously bequeathed to the poor, but whic
it was deemed advisable to invest in this manner together with th
addition of two other sums that were necessary to complete the amoun
required, as will be seen by the following list, viz. :—Mrs. Phillips, £5
Captain Broughton, £5; Mrs. Catherine Phillips, £10, all of Gwernhaylod
Mrs. Beatrice Lloyd, £20; Mrs. Margaret Lloyd, £10; Mr. John Hanmei
£10, all of Halghton; Mr. Edw. Shone, of Argoed, £10 and two sum
to make up; timber sold, £19 8s.; and donation of Mr. Thos. Lloyc
£10 12s., making in all £100.   The trustees of the fund are the Rectc
and Churchwardens, and the owners of Gwernhaylod, Bryn-y-pys, an
Maesguaelod.   By a deed bearing date 1732, it is stated that " The rent
are to be laid out in the clothing of poor people who shall be legall
settled and dwell within the parish of Overton, or such of them as sha

appear to be in greatest want thereof, whether men, women, or childre
or to what purposes the said trustees, or some of them, shall, from ti
to time think most proper and convenient." The rent is now £12 1
The garden and quillet in Penley were allotted to the parish of Pen
by the Commissioners for Inclosing Waste Land, and the cottage there
followed in right of the land. The two together bring in 10s. 6d. a yea

As to the disposal of the funds of the charity up to 1851 the mor
coming from both funds was distributed according to the terms of
deed relating solely to the land in Penley, viz. :—to such persons only
belonged to and lived in the parish of Overton. But at that time it v
thought well to extend the benefits to such persons as lived in the par
though they might not have a legal claim as parishioners. It will be s
that while the funds arising from the Penley trust must be spent
clothing, no such restriction applies to those of the Maes-y-Bartys la
which may be applied in any direction for the good of the poor.

A second charity, is the Bread Charity, or Thomas and Marga
Eyton's Trust. The name Eyton was long a very influential name in
district. Once the whole country from Bangor to Erbistock, we are t
belonged to the family. The two mentioned above, according to
returns, left, in the year 1786, some land to the Minister and Chur
wardens of Overton in trust to the poor, whether by note or deed, or
what period does not appear. Thomas Eyton died about the year 16
and Margaret Eyton about 1710, and the will of the latter is da
January 16th, 1709. She left one cottage and two parcels of land,
rent of which was to be devoted to the purchase of twelve penny loa
to the use and benefit of the poor of the parish of Overton Madoc.

also left two shillings to be distributed to the poor yearly on Margaret day, being the 28th of July, the produce of a bond due to her, as well a a penny dole, at her funeral. The cottage and land, included what use to be known as the "Church Field" in Cloy, formerly in the holding Lord Mostyn. Thomas Eyton's bequest, together with this provide twenty-four penny loaves for the poor. According to the bequest-board the church, Thomas Eyton left £2 12s. for bread, 4s. for a sermon on A Saints's Day, and 4s. annually for whipping dogs out of church, tl total amount realising £5 12s. When Lord Mostyn's sale took place 1848 the funds stopped, but after a great deal of communication with tl Charity Commissioners a compromise was arranged, whereby £183 12 was paid by the owner of the estate, and was laid out in the purcha: of £197 3s. in 3 per cent. consols, which now brings in £5 12s. annual to the trustees of the charity, the Rector and Churchwardens. Instea however, of twenty-four penny loaves, thirteen widows receive thirtee two-penny loaves every Sunday.

Having now considered the Lloyd and Eyton charities, which a: best known as the Flannel and Bread charities, we may come nearer o own time and see how those who have died not very long ago provide for the needy in the parish. But before looking into these matters, noti should be taken of the Ruabon charity, which derives its income fro the Gwallia farm in this parish. "Some time ago, about the year 1687, Mrs. Jane Hughes of Llanerchrugog, left £200 to be disposed of in : white gowns for the poor of Ruabon. This £200 produces an annuity £9 per annum, purchased by Sir John Wynn, Bart., and Ellis Lloyd, Esc issuing out of lands in Knolton, in the parish of Overton, now belongii

to E. Peel, Esq. of Bryn-y-pys. This is now distributed by Sir W.
Wynn, Bart., heir to the surviving trustee."   I believe the " wl
gowns " have given way to ordinary flannel.

Three good people lately have left legacies intentionally or practic
for the good of Overton.   The first to be noticed is F. R. Price, E
Before his death he intended to make an assignment by way of end
ment for the good of the schools of £280, which was a debt to him fr
the parish, but he died before he could execute it.   His executors d
up an agreement that what Mr. Price had intended should be carried i
force, and assigned the bond of £280 to the late Rector of Bangor-c
Overton and his successors, for the good of the parochial schools, in
year 1854.   This debt was disallowed at a vestry meeting in 1875,
consequently since then none of that endowment has been enjoyed
the schools.

While on the subject of the school we must remember the
Miss Mary Ann Bennion, to whose charity we owe the schoolmast
house, which was given by her in the year 1852, in consideration of
paid to her.   But the name of Bennion claims our notice by the gift
three alms-houses to the parish. This was in the year 1848.   The foll
ing inscription appears over the doorway :—" A.D. 1848.   These al
houses were erected to the memory of Caroline Bennion (late of Wrexh
fechan) by her affectionate sisters.   Faithful in the remitting exercis
charity to the poor and every Christian virtue.   She departed this life
the 6th of February, 1847."   The persons entitled to have one of th
three alms-houses are widows of Overton, 60 years of age, belonging to
Church of England, and regular attendants at Church and the H

Communion. The trustees were originally Lord Kenyon and the the:
Rector of Bangor ; and the will provides that whoever enjoys these title
are to be trustees, but there is some doubt now as to the true trusteeship

The last charity to be noticed is that of Mrs. F. R. Price (Elizabet]
Partridge Price), who bequeathed "to the Clothing Club at Overton, i:
the county of Flint, the sum of £100." This is now in the hands of th
Charity Commissioners, who pay to the trustees, the Rector and Church
wardens, three per cent interest per annum. The will is dated Augus
3rd, 1870.

Perhaps under the head of charities may be included the school c
the parish, and therefore I add in this chapter an account of the state c
education in this village. In the year 1847, an enquiry was set on foo
by the Government into all the schools, elementary and more advanced
in the country ; and from the report of the Commissioner of Wales w
gather what it is possible to find. He says the village contained 1,66
inhabitants, and that English was spoken by everyone. He was strucl
by the number of private schools, and he supposes it was so becaus
there was no really good elementary school with efficient teachers to b
found. There was Mr. Pickering's school with twenty-six children
Mrs. Hughes's (established since 1817) with twenty children ; Mr. Parry'
with six children ; and Lightwood Green School with fourteen children
But besides these private schools, there was a free school (which, howevei
had no endowment), established in 1811, where there were 123 childrei
on the books. The master was a soldier, and was the postmaster of th
village. He reports what happened at his inspection :—" Twenty-thre
can read, ten are learning to write, two can work a sum in simpl

addition.   Their knowledge of the sacred books is better, but only two answer questions in the Old Testament.   One boy when asked who was the first king of Israel replied 'John.'"   He describes the system of teaching.   It is decidedly antiquated.   In arithmetic for instance, which is professed by several boys, he dictates each step to a whole class, who repeat it after him in a chanting tone, thus :—" About an inch from the top and an inch from the left hand side set down seven;" and then he continues, " about half an inch to the right set down six."   But if the pupils were asked to put down seventy-six on their slates, they would be perfectly unable to do so.

It was time therefore that something should be done, and so in 1848 the present girls' and boys' school was built for boys, and girls, and infants.   The whole was paid for by subscription, and the accounts were published in 1853, showing that £361 8s. was paid for the whole.   It seems to have been in the main the energy of the late Rev. H. O. Wrench, which brought the building to so successful an issue, while the well-known liberality of Mr. Peel appears in the front of the list.   In 1852, Miss Mary Ann Bennion, in consideration of £5 paid to her, handed over to the trustees of the school the house, to be for ever appropriated and used for a residence of the schoolmaster.   That house was on the site of the old school, which had been granted by Mr. F. R. Price of Bryn-y-pys, in 1817 or 1818.   The present infant school was added in 1874, on the recommendation of H.M. Inspector.   Since then a lavatory and cloak room have been added by the generosity of Mrs. Peel of Bryn-y-pys.

The school was united to the " Incorporated National Society " in

April, 1853, a sum of £40 having been granted by the National Societ
towards erecting the school premises. It was placed under Governmen
Inspection in June, 1867, as a mixed school (i.e. boys and girls taugh
together) with only 25 scholars, there being still so large a number c
" private schools " in the village. In 1878, the boys and girls wer
separated, and the infants taught with the girls. The first report wa
issued in February, 1868.

Chapter VII.

Ube Traditions and Customs of Overton.

CCORDING to old tradition Overton Churchyard is on
the Seven Wonders of North Wales.   The doggerel w
states this exists in two forms, one version runs thus c
ting Overton—

> Gresford bells and Wrexham steeple,
> Llangollen vale and all the people.

Another version is as follows:—

> Pistyll Rhaiadr and Wrexham steeple,
> Snowdon's mountain without its people,
> Overton churchyard and St. Winifred's wells,
> Llangollen bridge and Gresford bells.

" Ill-natured people say that it is due to a local joke that n
Overton churchyard a 'Wonder.'"   The following is the story:—"

a year or two ago there grew a small yew tree within the turret on tl
tower, and it was a constant puzzle to those who visited the church
see the grand yew trees, to know how many yews there were, though th
might count over and over again the number was not right, as th
omitted the one on the tower." This little tree has now disappeared
its roots were eating into the stone work, and so it had to be destroyed.

Now that we are speaking of the church tower the custom of tl
curfew bell should be mentioned. Most people know the origin of tl
name ; it is from *Couvre feu*, two French words, meaning to all inter
"put the fire out," because the bell used to be rung at a particular tin
to warn people of the danger of fire to their old houses of wood. Curfe
bells are rung at different times in different places. In Overton it is rui
at 8 p.m. between the 5th of November and the 2nd of February. /
Chester and elsewhere it is rung all the year round at 9 p.m. There ma
have been some worthy who so arranged our system as to make it usef
at some time, though that use is obsolete. There is another bell rung
8 a.m. every Sunday to let people know that the service will be held
usual.

I have found that the name "Mayors of the Green" was a title fo
the head for the time being, of a drinking club, an office answering to tl
"Lord of Misrule" in the olden time. This club had its head quarters :
the Bowling Green Inn. Membership was gained by being able to qua
at a single draught a cup (of ale or wine) of a certain size. Those wl
were able to do this were called Freemen. There is at Gwernhaylod tl
mayor's chair, with a date upon it, and Mr. Fletcher has in his possessic
the qualification cup and the book in which were entered the names

the members, amongst whom most of the leading gentry of the neighbour
hood appear.   Mention is made in an old account of rural sports at Mold
of mayors and sheriffs of the sports, so that the name was of the principa
at the head of these things.   We may be thankful that Overton is no
now the centre of such a revolting and degrading custom, but confines it
interest to lawn tennis and cricket.

Some reminiscences of the old bridge may be interesting, which hav
been communicated by two old inhabitants who have known Overton fo
nearly 80 years.   The present bridge was built about the year 1814, an
there are at least two old natives of Overton who remember its bein
erected.

It was originally intended to have been of one arch like the celebrate
Grosvenor bridge at Chester, but apparently the architect had not th
cunning or knowledge to create such a work, as when several courses c
stones had been laid on each side, the supports gave way, and the whol
fell into the river.   Thus the first design could not be carried out, and th
present bridge of two arches, which is a fine structure in its way, wa
built.   The name of the architect was Penson, and he designed the nortl
aisle of Overton Church shortly afterwards.   He also contracted for th
memorial of the jubilee of George III., on Moel Fammau, which wa
erected in 1813.

The description of the old bridge we give in the words of an ol
inhabitant.   "The old bridge at Overton was so narrow that two cart
could not pass on it, and so low that when the river was swollen a mai
could dip his hand into the water from the top of it.   It was some fev
yards higher up the river than the present bridge, as the foundation

when the river is low, very clearly show. It had on each side a lc
wooden rail, which we called the battlement. The approach each wa
was down a steep hill. On the Denbighshire side the turn of the road :
the end of the bridge formed a sharp angle." The same continues, "
once saw the leaders of the stage coach in making the turn, run with the
forelegs over the rail, and I have heard old people say they could rememb
the coach, horses, and passengers and all, once fall over into the rive
but I cannot say if anyone was drowned. I have also heard from tl
same people that, during a great flood, the mill a little higher up the rive
being at the time a low thatched building, was washed down by 'tl
fresh' and that the roof floated down the river, and striking one of tl
arches of the bridge, destroyed it." Another account from the celebrate
sporting writer, Nimrod, says, "The driver had his box coat on, and tl
river was swollen by the rain, so that his life must have been lost had n
a fisherman been passing accidentally in his coracle and picked him up.'

Pennant in his *Tours* makes this statement about the old bridge: "Tl
bridge consists of two neat arches, and was first built of stone by tl
munificence of Gwenhwyvar, daughter of Jerwerth Ddu, of Pengwern, ne
Llangollen, a maiden lady who resided at Eyton with her sister Margare
who was married to Madoc ap Evan Eyton."

In *The Grael* is a statement in Welsh, that Overton Bridge was bu
by Gwenhwyvar, the wife of David Holbache. The date is given th
"14...," whence it would appear to have been partially obliterated in t
MS. from which the statement is derived.

David Holbache was steward of Oswestry and M.P. for Shropshi
early in the 15th century, and in 1407 founded Oswestry School (in cc

junction with his wife). She was of Sweeney, the daughter of Jevon
John ap Eynon.

There is still extant a picture of this bridge, which it is hoped may
preserved amongst the relics of the past history of the parish.

We cannot leave the neighbourhood of Overton bridge without relati
two stories which must be ever connected with that hill on the Flintsh
side, which is commonly called Gwall Hill.   Both of them we have hea
from the same old friends mentioned before.   The first is that abo
seventy years ago a snake, evidently of some considerable size, was se
by a carter who had charge of a team of horses coming up the hill.
came out of the hedge on the left side, and struck at the foremost of t
team, and was with some difficulty killed by the man.   Its length was su
that when placed upon the cart full of coals, its head reached the grou
in front, while its tail trailed on the ground at the back !   The seco
story is of later date.   In the late Francis Richard Price's day, an ala
was once raised that the colliers of Ruabon, who were on strike, intend
to march in a body to Bryn-y-pys, and to demolish it ! The Flintsh
Yeomanry, of which Mr. Price was the Colonel, were called out, and w
great pomp and show took up a position at the top of the Gwall H
Suffice it to say that the colliers never came, and the gallant horsem
returned to Overton unwounded but crest-fallen.   This circumstance h
been immortalised by some lines written at the time, entitled " T
Battle of Gwall Hill. "

The volunteers of 1803, were partly Infantry and partly Cavalry.   T
Cavalry were commanded by Colonel Puleston ; the Infantry by Colo
George, Lord Kenyon.   The officers were gazetted between 1803-18

On June 23rd, 1804, the Cavalry had a field day at Lightwood Green, and were presented with Colours; after which the four troops marched to Overton, and drank the king's health, and were dismissed.

There is a field a little east of the church called Prison Bars Field, and the origin of its name is I should think to be found in this : On the 12th August, 1820, a game of Prison Base was played between the young men of Overton and those of Hanmer, which was decided in favour of the former, they gaining eleven ticks, while the Hanmer men gained only five. Lord Kenyon gave a prize of two guineas to the winners.

I now come to a custom in some ways peculiar to Overton (which is really of ancient origin, I believe), of going round "souling" on the day after All Saints' Day. The meaning of that word souling is to be found in the day itself, which is All Souls' Day, and probably when this custom first arose those who besieged the houses of the rich came for the purpose of entreating the prayers of men for the souls of the dead, who were, they believed, then in Purgatory enduring the punishment due to them for their sinful lives. Speaking seriously, therefore, the " souling " of the past was a religious office, and meant a great deal; for however we may view that doctrine of which it was the outcome, it was with earnest feeling that the " soulers " walked about the country asking for the prayers of men. However, that idea vanished at the time, I suppose, of the Reformation, and now all that remains is a doggerel with little rhyme or reason in it. I give what seem to be the words that are used in Overton :—

> A soul! a soul! an apple or two;
> If you have no apple, a pear will do;
> A plum or a cherry
> To make us all merry.

> I pray you, good lady, a soul cake,
> The roads are very dirty, my shoes are very thin,
> I've got a little pocket to put a penny in.
> > Go down to your cellar,
> > Your cellar goes deep;
> By walkin' and talkin' you'll get a good name;
> I hope, you good mistress, you'll never deny !
> > One for Peter, two for Paul,
> > Three for the man that made us all.
> Up with the kettle, and down with the pan,
> Give us an answer and we'll be gan."

In the lines there are some that rhyme, but many do not; and as the sense it will baffle most investigation. "Soul cakes" have been long an institution connected with the day, and, I suppose, may ra with the barbarous "hot cross buns" of Good Friday.

This doggerel is found with differences at Malpas, Mow Cop, a Oswestry; at the latter place the most complete version which is kno is in vogue. At Malpas the children "soul" in the morning, the men the evening, the latter having a different set of words. The sai mentioned are the same in all versions—Peter and Paul. I suppose tl are chosen because to men's minds these two were the two chiefs; as have in an old proverb, "Robbing Peter to pay Paul," which seems betray an idea of right and wrong, which is anything but the true o And for this reason, too, we find that churches in old time were for most part dedicated to St. Peter or St. Paul, or to the Holy Trinity.

CHAPTER VIII.

𝕿𝖍𝖊 𝖔𝖑𝖉 𝕱𝖆𝖒𝖎𝖑𝖎𝖊𝖘 𝖔𝖋 𝕺𝖛𝖊𝖗𝖙𝖔𝖓.

OVERTONS OF OVERTON.

David Fychan of the Wern, it the parish of Hanmer.
|
Jenkyn ab David of the Wern.
|
David of Dungrey.   Gruffydd.
|
Gruffydd Fychan of Overton Madog.
|
John Overton of Overton Madog.
|
Thomas Overton=Harriett Alswood.
|
Beatrix=Edward Lloyd of Halghton.   Mary=Edward Phillips of Gwernhaylod.

FLETCHERS OF GWERNHAYLOD.

Y Badi alias Madoc ap Howel temp. Hen. VII. (?)

Philip of Gwernhaylod.

Edward ap Philip of Gwernhaylod.

Edward Phillips of Gwernhaylod.

Edward Phillips of Gwernhaylod═daughter of John Hanmer of Bradenheath.

William Phillips

Edward Phillips═Mary daughter of Thomas Overton.

William Phillips═Anne, daughter of Captain Broughton of Mardwiel.

Mary, born 1661═Thomas Lloyd of Halghton.   Katherine.

Thomas Lloyd═Alice Cleveland,   Mary Lloyd of Gwernhaylod═Rev. John Fletcher of Strudda Bank, co. Cumberland. Rector of Hawarden and Bangorisy coed

Phillips Lloyd Fletcher═Eleanor Wynne of Llwyn.

Capt. P. L. Fletcher.   Capt. John Fletcher.   Major Thomas Fletcher.   Rev. Lloyd Fletcher.   Mary═Capt. Walker.   Eleanor═Capt. Tringham

Phillips Lloyd Fletcher of Nerquis, Gwernhaylod, and Pengwern.   Thomas Hanmer Fletcher.   Frederick Lloyd Fletcher.   Wm. Lloyd Tringham.

Llewellyn Walker Howel Tringham.   Mostyn Frederick Lloyd Tringham

PRICE OF BRYNYPYS.

Rys.

David ap Rys.

Rys ap David. Thomas Prys of Bryn-y-pys.

Price of Bryn-y-pys. William.

Thomas.

John Price. Richard Price of Ballyhooly=Grand-daughter of Dr. Parry, Bishop of Killaloe.

1710. Francis Price of Bryn-y-pys=Alice, daugther of John Cleveland of Birkenhead (widow of Thomas Lloyd of Gwernhaylod).

Richard Price=1st, Dorothea.=2nd, Anne Puleston of Emral.
(Assumed the name of Parry in consequence of a bequest from Hon. Benj. Parry, P.C. of Ireland.

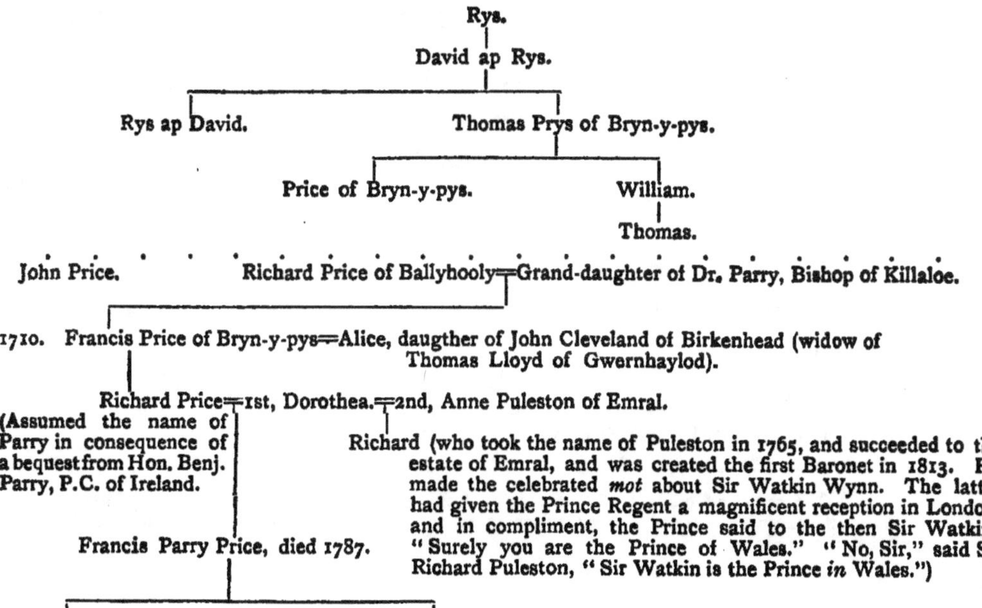

Richard (who took the name of Puleston in 1765, and succeeded to the estate of Emral, and was created the first Baronet in 1813. He made the celebrated *mot* about Sir Watkin Wynn. The latter had given the Prince Regent a magnificent reception in London, and in compliment, the Prince said to the then Sir Watkin, "Surely you are the Prince of Wales." "No, Sir," said Sir Richard Puleston, "Sir Watkin is the Prince *in* Wales.")

Francis Parry Price, died 1787.

Francisca=George Kenyon of Cefn. Francis Richard Price, died 1853. Sold Bryn-y-pys.

Pulestons of Emral, Lightwood, and Overton.

Roger Puleston of Emral, died 1479.

Philip Puleston, 1535=Ellen daughter David ap Rys.

Richard Puleston of Overton Madoc=Catherine daughter of Robert ap David of Overton ap David of Madoc, &c.

John Puleston of Pickhill.   Richard.   Thomas.   Roger.   Edward.

Thomas=Elizabeth Salusbury of Erbistock (great-grand-daughter of Thomas Grosvenor of Eaton.)

John.

John.

John, inherited Emral, died 1735.

Thomas (died 1768).   John.   Anna=Richard Parry Price, F.R.S., of Bryn-y-pys.

Leyland says :—" Edward Pilston sonne to ye knight dweleith in Overtone Paroche at Coitegelli." I cannot find this place.

The Old Families of Overton.

Eyton of Maesgwaelod.

(A branch of the great family of Eyton of Eyton).

David Eyton of Eyton Uchaf.

Sir Robert Eyton, Priest of Overton Madoc.

John Eyton of Maesgwaelod.

James Eyton (who had land in Gwalliau).

Richard Eyton of Gwalliau.

Randle Eyton of Maesgwaelod.

Thomas Eyton of Maesgwaelod=Catherine, daughte
                      Humphrey Elli
                      Allthrey.

Appendix I.

Overton Charters.

CHARTER ROLL EDW. I., No. 23.

Pro Roberto de Creuequeor — Rex Archiepiscopis etc. salutem Sciatis nos concessisse et hac carta nostra con firmasse dilecto et fideli nostro Roberto de Creuequer, quod ipse et heredes su imperpetuum habeant unum mercatum singulis septimanis per diem mercuri apud manerium suum de Ouerton in partibus de Mailors ei seneyk in Wallia et vnam feriam ibidem singulis annis per xv. dies duraturam videlicet in vigilia in die et in crastino Nativitati Beatæ Mariæ virginis et per duodecim dies sequentes, nisi mercatum illud et feria illa sin ad nocumentum vicinorum mercatorum et vicinarum feriarum Quare volumus et firmite precipimus pro nobis et heredibus nostris quod predictus Robertus et heredes sui imper petuum habeant predicta mercatum et feriam apud manerium suum predictum c omnibus libertatibus et liberis consuetutinibus ad huiusmodi mercatum et feriam per tinentibus, nisi mercatum illud et feria illa sint ad nocumentum vicinorum mercatorum e vicinarum feriarum sicut prædictum est. Hiis testibus venerabili patre R. Bathoniens et Wellensi Episcopo G. de Clar' Comite Gloucestriæ et Hertfordiæ Rogero le Bigo Comite Norfolciæ et Marescallo Angliæ Henrico de Lacy Comite Lincolniæ Hugone fili Ottonis Waltero de Helyun Roberto filio Johannis Patricio de Cadurt' Ricardo de Bosc et aliis Datum per manum nostram apud Westmonasterium vij die Julij.

Overton Charters.

CHARTER ROLL 20 EDW. I. No. 55.

Pro hominibus | Rex Archiepiscopis etc, salutem Sciatis quod volumus et concedimus
 de Ouerton | nobis et hæredibus nostris quod villa nostra de Ouerton decetero
Burgus sit et homines nostri eiusdem ville liberi sint Burgenses et quod ipsi et hæi
sui mesuagia sua infra Burgum prædictum imperpetuum habeant et teneant de r
et hæredibus nostris per seruicia inde debita et consueta—concessimus eciam eis
Burgensibus quod de se ipsis eligant singulis annis tres probos et legalles homines e
Ballivo nostro ibidem qui pro tempore fuerit in proximo Hundredo nostro post fe:
Sancti Michaelis presentent qui unum ex ipsis tribus eligat, et preficiat Ballivum nos
ville prædictæ qui sacramentum prestabit coram eodem Ballivo de hüs que ad Balli
eiusdem villæ pertinent facienda et fideliter exequenda Volumus eciam et concedimus
prædicti Burgenses habeant liberam prisonam suam in Burgo prædicto de omr
transgressoribus suis ibidem, volumus eciam et concedimus, quod si aliquis dicto
Burgensorum aliquid fecerit in eodem Burgo contra coronam nostram quod non d
minetur in aliquo loco nisi infra libertatem villæ prædictæ coram justiciario n
verumptamen, si aliqui dictorum Burgensorum rectati accusati vel indictari fuerint s
aliqua transgressione vbi non fuerit periculum amissionis vitæ vel membrorum in huius:
casibus volumus quod ea occasione imprisonentur quamdiu bonam et sufficie:
manucaptionem invenerint ad standum inde recto coram capitali justiciario nostro vel
justiciariis nostris ad hoc deputatis concessimus insuper eisdem Burgensibus quod o1
terræ eidem Burgo iam assignate de warennate et deafforestate sint omnino infra libt
villæ prædictæ. Et qd judei in eodem Burgo non morentur aliquibus temporibus
cedimus eciam pro nobis et heredibus nostris eisdem Burgensibus libertates subscr
videlicet quod nullus vicecomitum nostrorum in aliquo se intromittat super eos de a
placito vel querela vel occasione vel aliqua re alia ad predictam villam pertinente n
defectum Burgensium prædictorum ant Ballivorum suorum. Et quod ipsi habeant gi
mercatoriam cum Hansa et aliis consuetudinibus et libertatibus ad gildam illam pertinen!
Ita, quod nullus qui non sit de gilda illa, mercandisam aliquam faciat in eadem villa, ni
voluntate Burgensium prædictorum concedimus eciam eisdem, quod si aliquis nativus ali(
in p'fata villa manserit et terram in eadem tenuerit, et fuerit in prædicta villa, et Hansa et]
et Scoth' cum eisdem hominibus nostris per unum annum et unum diem sine calun

deinceps non possit repeti a domino suo, set in aedem villa liber permaneat Item volumus et concedimus, quod Burgenses nostri quieti sint per totam terram nostram de theloneo stallagio, lastagio, passagio, muragio, pontagio et ostallagio et de Danegeld et Gaijwijt et omnibus aliis consuetudinibus et exaccionibus per totam potestatem nostram tam in Anglia, quam in omnibus aliis terris nostris et quod ipsi vel corum bona vbicunque locorum in terra vel potestate nostra inuenta non arrestentur pro aliquo debito de quo fidei fussores aut principales debitores non exbiterint. Nisi forte ipsi debitores de eorum sint communa et potestate habentes, vnde de debitis suis in toto vel in parte satisfacere possint et ipsi Burgensis per quos Burgus ille regitur eis in justicia defuerint et quod dicti Burgenses nostri pro transgressione seu forisfactura servientum suorum catalla et bona sua in manibus ipsorum inventa aut alicubi locorum per ipsos servientes depenita quatenus sua esse sufficienter probare poterunt, non amittant, concedimus eciam quod si idem Burgenses aut eorum aliqui infra terram aut potestatem nostram testati vel intestati decesserint nos vel heredes nostri bona ipsorum confiscari non faciemus quin eorum heredes aut executores ea integre habeant. Et volumus quod Burgenses nostri villæ prædictæ in omnibus sint adeo liberi quod nullus Ballivus extraneus aliquam habeat potestatem infra libertatem villæ prædictæ ad aliquam districtionem faciendam et quod nullus eorum cogatur accomodare Ballivo suo vltra duodecim denarios contra voluntatem suam. Quare volumus et firmiter precipimus pro nobis et heredibus nostris, quod villa nostra de Ouerton' decetero liber Burgus sit et quod homines nostri eiusdem villæ liberi sint Burgenses, et quod ipsi et heredes sui mesuagia sua infra Burgum prædictum imperpetuum habeant et teneant de nobis et heredibus nostris per servicia inde debita et consueta et quod prædicti Burgenses nostri et successores sui habeant et teneant omnes libertates quietancias et liberas consuetudines superius expressas sine occasione vel impedimento nostri vel heredum nostrorum Ballinorum seu Ministrorum nostrorum quorumcunque imperpetuum. Hiis testibus venerabilibus patribus R. Bathoniensi et Wellensi J. Wyntoniensi A. Dunolmensi W. Elyensi Episcopis Edmundo fratre nostro Willelmo de Valenc' avunculo nostro, Henrico de Lacy Comite Lincolniæ, Humfrido de Bohun Comite Herefordiæ et Essexiæ, Reginaldo de Grey Roberto Tibotot Waltero de Bello Campo et aliis Datum per manum nostram apud Westmonasterium xx° die Januarij.

CONFIRMATION OF FOREGOING CHARTER BY RICHARD II.

RICHARD by the grace of God King of England & France & Lord of Ire
to all Archbishops Bishops Abbots Priors Dukes. Earls Viscounts Ba:
Judges Mayors Ministers Bailiffs & to all His loving subjects se1
greeting. We have examin'd a Charter wch. His Majesty King Edwa
famous memory our most honoured grandfather granted in these w
Edward by the grace of God King of England Lord of Ireland & Du
Aquitaine to all Archbishops Bishops Abbots Priors Dukes Earls Viscounts Barons Jv
Mayors Ministers Bailiffs & all his loving subjects sendeth greeting. Be it known
all men that it is our Royal Will & Pleasure. & we do hereby declare for our sel1
Heirs & Successors, that our village of Overton for the future be a free Burrough & tha
subjects, inhabitants of the said Burrough, be free Burgesses. & that their Hei:
successors should hold their messuages within their said Burrough, of us our Hei
successors, for ever, paying their customary rights & dues. We have granted lik(
unto our said Burgesses power of chusing out of their own Body every year three
good & true, & shall present them to our Bailiff of the Next Hundred, the day afte
Feast of St. Michael, who shall chuse one of the three & make Him Bailiff of the Vi
afores^d. who shall swear before the said Bailiff that He will duly & truly execute the (
of Bailiff of the said Village. It is also our Royal will & pleasure that the afor(
Burgesses have liberty of erecting a Prison within the Burrough afore^sd, for all
criminals, & we likewise ordain that if any of the Burgesses. afore^sd, comit any off(
against our Crown & Dignity that He shall not be confined anywhere but within
liberties of the said Burrough. Notwithstanding if any of the Burgesses afore^sd be acc
or indicted of any crime, wherein Life or Limb is not concernd Our Pleasure is that in t
cases they should be imprisoned till they find good & sufficient security that they
answer it before Our Lord Chief Justice or any other our Judges appointed for the try
such causes. We farther will & comand that all lands of the said Burroughs design
Warrens or Forrest, should be deemed to be within the liberties of the said Village &
our Judges sh^ld not continue any time within ye said Burrough. We likewise grant for
self & successors the privilledges hereafter mentiond viz that none of our Lord lieuter
should concern Himself in any Plea or complaint relating to ye said Village unle

happen thro the default of yᵉ said Burgesses or their Bailiffs. And that they should have a Mercantile Gild with all the Privilledges and imunities belonging to such a Society, & that none but members of that Society presume to make any Merchandise within yᵉ said Village unless by yᵉ consent of the Burgesses aforeˢᵈ. We likewise ordain that if any inhabitant of any other Lᵈship shall settle in yᵉ said Village & occupie lands there & there continue for one year or a day & pay scot and lot as others of our said Village do, without any disturbance, that He shall not be liable to be demanded by His former Lᵈ but shall for ever continue free of yᵉ sᵈ Village. It is also our Royal Will & pleasure that ye Burgesses of yᵉ sᵈ Burrough, sᵘ be exempted from all manner of Tolls whatever, Customs and Tributes as well in all other our Dominions as in our Kᵐ of England and yᵗ neither they nor their goods, in whatever part of our Dominions they shall be found, sᵘ be liable to be arrested for any debt, in which yʸ are not either Principals or Sureties, unless yᵉ debtors themselves have it in their power to satisfie their debts in whole or in part, and that yᵉ Burgesses themselves, by whom that Burrough is governed, have been wanting in doing them justice. And that our Burgesses aforeˢᵈ shall not forfeit their goods & Chattels for any fault or misdemeanour of yʳ servants, whether they be found in yʳ servants keeping or disposed of by them anywhere else, in case they can prove yᵐ to be yʳ own property. We also will or command y if any of our Burgesses aforesᵈ shall die within our Dominions, either with or without a will that His goods shall not be forfeited either to us or our Heirs but His Heirs or Executors sᵘ enjoy them entirely. Our Will and pleasure also is, yᵗ our Burgesses of our Borrough aforesᵈ sᵈ be so free, yᵗ no Bailiff shall have any power of making any distress within y liberties of yᵉ sᵈ Burrough & yᵗ none of them sᵘ be obliged to pay yᵉ Bailiff above twelve pence, unless it be wᵗʰ His own consent. Wherefore our Royal will and pleasure is, that our Burrough of Overton for yᵉ tuture be a free Burrough, & our subjects of yᵉ sᵈ Burrʰ be free Burgesses & yᵗ they and yʳ Heirs hold all yʳ Messuages wᵗʰn yᵉ sᵈ Burrʰ of us & our Heirs for ever paying their antient & customary rights and dues, and yᵗ our Burgesses aforesᵈ yʳ Heirs & successors sᵈ have & enjoy all yᵉ privilledges & imunities aforesᵈ wᵗʰout any let or Hinderance of us or our Heirs our Bailiffs or Ministers whatever.

Witnesses Rich Bath & Wells. Thos Winton Ed Ely Edm our Bro Willᵐ of Valence our Uncle, Lacy Earl of Lincoln, Humʸ Bohun Earl of Hereford & Yo Regin Grey Bol (illegible). Walter Beauchamp and others. Given under our hand at Westmin Jan 20ᵗʰ in yᵉ 20ᵗʰ year of our Reign.

We also by these presents do ratify and confirm all yᵉ grants of our G father to oᵘ beloved burgesses of yᵉ Burrough, of Overton aforesᵈ, & all yʳ Heirs and successors coᵗ tained in yᵉ Charter aforesᵈ. As they and their Predecessors have had and enjoyed liberties aforesᵈ yʳᵉ venerable persons being witness yᵉ Arch B of Canterʸ Primate of ᵃ England, our Chancellor H Lincoln, & Ro London, Jⁿᵒ Warren E of Guise, Wᵐ Bohun of Northampton, Hen of Lancas E of Derby, W Clinton E of Huntingdon Hen ᴸ (illegible) J Darcy our Cosin, Governor of our Hospital and others, given under our Haɪ at Westminᵗʳ May yᵉ 8ᵗʰ in yᵉ 14ᵗʰ year of our reign over England & over France. We fiɪ confirming those grants & privilledges for ourselves our Heirs & successors as far as us lies, do ratifie & establish yᵐ as they are contained in yᵉ Charter aforesᵈ. And moreov being desirious of doing yᵐ a greater favor, we do ordain for ourselves & successors as f as in us lies, yᵗ altho they or yʳ Predecessors of yᵉ Burrʰ of Ourton aforesᵈ sˡˡ not haᵛ enjoyed any or all of yᵉ Privilledges granted in yᵉ Charter aforesᵈ yᵗ if they yʳ Heirs aɪ Successors being Burgesses of yᵉ Village aforesᵈ sˡˡ enjoy all yᵉ rights privilledges imunities for yᵉ future wᵗʰout any let or hindrance of us our Heirs, successors, or Judgᵉ Ecclesiasticks, Sheriffs or any of our Bailiffs or Ministers wᵗever.

And we farther grant out of our Royal favour for ourselves and successors as far as in ᵘ lies unto yᵉ Burr aforesᵈ sll not be liable to be comitted by any forreigners wᵗever, in casᵉ of appeals accusations indictments or demands already imposed, or to be impos'd upon ᵞ wᵗʰ in the County of Flynt at any time, but only by yᵉ Burgess of yᵉ Burr aforesᵈ ᵃ by English Burgessˢ of yᵉ County of Flynt. These venerable persons being witnessᵉ yᵉ Arch B of Canter Primate of all England, our Chancellor of Exon Lᵈ Treasurer Jⁿᵒ Kiɪ of Castile & Lyons, D of Lancaster, & Edm E of Cambridge, Thos of Woodstock E Buckingⁿ our Beloved Uncle, Richᵈ Arundel, Tho Beauchamp E of Warwick, Willia Beauchamp our (omitted). Hugh Segrave governⁿ of our Hospital J Lᵈ Fordham Keep of yᵉ Privy Seal & others given under our hands at Westminster yᵉ 22ⁿᵈ of May in yᵉ ᵴ year of our Reign.

By a brief under yᵉ Privy Seal & yᵉ Payment of six Marks at Flynt, into yᵉ Staɪ Office. WALTHAM.

Inroll'd before William E' of Suffolk our Lᵈ Chief Justice of Chester on Friday neᵊ preceding yᵉ feast of St Michael yᵉ Arch Angel in yᵉ twenty second year of yᵉ Reign Henry yᵉ 6th.

The Cycle.

It is only right that some mention should be made of the Cycle Clu
which often had its meetings in Overton, in days gone by. The followir
account has been most kindly furnished by Miss Lloyd Fletcher of Ne
quis. In the *Cambrian Quarterly Magazine*, for April, 1829, it is state
that " the Cycle, now merely a social meeting, the members of whic
are gentlemen resident in the neighbourhood of Wrexham and part
Cheshire, was originally a secret assembly, which met for the purpose
furthering the pretensions of Prince Charles Edward to the crown
Great Britain." The earliest list of members is the following:—"Jan. 2
1721. We the underwitten promise to meet at the time and place to o
names respectively affixed, and do ratify the accustomed rules of tl
Society for the year ensuing, Watkin Williams Wynn, Eubule Lloy
William Edwards, Kenrick Eyton, Thomas Eyton, Robert Ellice, Joh
Robinson, Richard Clayton, Thomas Holland, Robert Davies, Joh
Puleston, George Shackerley." The following is the Cycle Song :—

I hope there's no soul
That o'er this bowl
But means honest ends to pursue,
With the voice go the heart,

The Cycle.

And let's never depart
From the faith of the honest true Blue.
CHORUS :
True Blue—from the faith of the honest, true Blue.

For country and friends,
Let us d——n private ends,
And keep old British virtue in view ;
Despising the tribe
Who are bought with a bribe,
Be honest to our true Blue, true Blue.

Here's a health to all those
Who slav'ry oppose
And our trade both defend and renew,
And to each honest voice
That concurs in the choice
And support of an honest true Blue, true Blue.

With hounds and with horn
We'll rise in the morn,
With vigor the chase to pursue ;
Corruption's the cry
We'll chase till we die,
Be honest, be ever true Blue, true Blue.

(Added in 1745).
For the days we've misspent
Let us truly repent,
And render to Cæsar his due ;
Here's a health to the lad
With his bonnet and plaid,
For the world cannot stain his true Blue, true Blue.

The way the members of the club drank the king's health was b
passing their glasses over the water jug, meaning "the king over th
water" (an exile).   The Welsh gentry were very loyal to the Stuarts.   I
most of the old houses may be seen a small picture of Charles Edwar(
and also snuff boxes in enamel with his portrait.   Lady Williams Wyn
has the Cycle jewel presented to a Lady Williams Wynn in 1781, a
patroness.   A white rose was the early badge of the Cycle.   The la:
secretary of the club was the Rev. Lloyd Wynne, some time in charg
of Overton Parish.

In the diary of Charlotte Williams Wynn, December 5, 1843, is a
entry stating "I am suffering from a bad headache to-day, the cons(
quence of a terribly hot dinner of thirty people last night, when a clu
called the Cycle held one of its meetings." This shows that then the Clu
had ceased to be a political one.